better together*

*This book is best read together, grownup and kid.

 akidsco.com

a
kids
book
about

a kids book about

surrogacy

by Kira Chesak

A Kids Co.
Editor Emma Wolf
Designer Rick DeLucco
Creative Director Rick DeLucco
Studio Manager Kenya Feldes
Sales Director Melanie Wilkins
Head of Books Jennifer Goldstein
CEO and Founder Jelani Memory

DK
Delhi Technical Team Bimlesh Tiwary Pushpak Tyagi, Rakesh Kumar
Senior Production Editor Jennifer Murray
Senior Production Controller Louise Minihane
Senior Acquisitions Editor Katy Flint
Acquisitions Project Editor Sara Forster
Managing Art Editor Vicky Short
Managing Director, Licensing Mark Searle

First American edition, 2025
Published in the United States by DK Publishing, 1745 Broadway, 20th Floor,
New York, NY 10019

First published in Great Britain in 2025 by
Dorling Kindersley Limited, 20 Vauxhall Bridge Road, London SW1V 2SA
A Penguin Random House Company

The authorised representative in the EEA is
Dorling Kindersley Verlag GmbH. Arnulfstr. 124, 80636 Munich, Germany

A catalog record for this book is available from the Library of Congress.
A CIP catalogue record for this book is available from the British Library.
ISBN: 978-0-2417-4378-2

DK books are available at special discounts when purchased in bulk for sales
promotions, premiums, fund-raising, or education use. For details, contact:
DK Publishing Special Markets, 1745 Broadway, 20th Floor, New York, NY 10019
SpecialSales@dk.com

Printed and bound in China
www.dk.com
akidsco.com

MIX
Paper | Supporting
responsible forestry
FSC™ C018179

This book was made with Forest
Stewardship Council™ certified
paper – one small step in DK's
commitment to a sustainable future.
**Learn more at www.dk.com/uk/
information/sustainability**

This book is dedicated to
my husband, Nick, my 3 kids,
Finnley, Beckett, and Evey,
and to my little surro babe:
thanks for being my belly buddy!

Intro
for grownups

Everyone is different and has a unique story. Some stories are sad, some are happy, and every story comes from an experience that makes us who we are today.

Infertility is a sad story, and it is often not talked about among grownups. There are some people who are unable to have babies, and if they want to have babies, they need help from others, like doctors, nurses, scientists, egg or sperm donors, or surrogates. With the help of those people, sometimes a sad story can become a happy story when the battle of infertility ends.

In this book, I tell my story (which, spoiler: has a happy ending)! I hope you are inspired to talk about what makes you different—your story is one worth telling! Learning more from the experience of other people helps our world become more knowledgeable, more understanding, more compassionate, and ultimately, more loving.

Hi!

My name is Kira.
And I've done a lot
of cool things in my life.

But one of the **most amazing** things I've done as a grownup is be a surrogate.

So, what is
a surrogate?

Well, a surrogate is someone who carries* a baby for someone else.

*And I don't mean hold the baby in your arms...more on that ater!

Sometimes, people who want to create a family using their own bodies can't, even though they want to.

In order to have a family,
some people choose adoption,
egg or sperm donation,
and some choose surrogacy.

And since I enjoyed being pregnant with my kids, I decided to help someone else grow their family through surrogacy.

I felt a calling to help in

in my heart
this way.

So you might be wondering, how does someone become a surrogate?

The first step, for me, was applying to an agency that does this work every single day.

They match people who want to have babies but can't, with people who can carry those babies for them.

When I was matched with a couple, I told my kids that we were going to help 2 people start a family, and that I would start getting my body ready to carry their baby.

My kids were pretty understanding about the whole process! We kept up a constant conversation in our house so they were always in the loop.

Then, I met with my doctor to make sure my body was ready to carry a baby.

And after that was done, we started writing a contract, which is a legal agreement to explain all the rules to follow during this process.

Our contract was over 20 pages long, so that's **a LOT** of rules!

Next was getting my body ready to carry the baby, which involved medications and a lot of help from doctors.

There was some easy medication, and there was some not-so-easy medication.

And all of it was new for me because I hadn't taken any medication during my previous pregnancies.

Getting shots is no fun at all, and I was doing it every day.

My husband helped me with the shots, and my doctor told us to imagine playing darts!

Playing darts
is more fun than
getting a shot,
but these shots

made m

e strong

enough to carry someone else's baby!

Some of the medication had side effects, but none of it stopped me from playing with my kids or living my life. And it was totally worth it knowing I was helping another family have a baby!

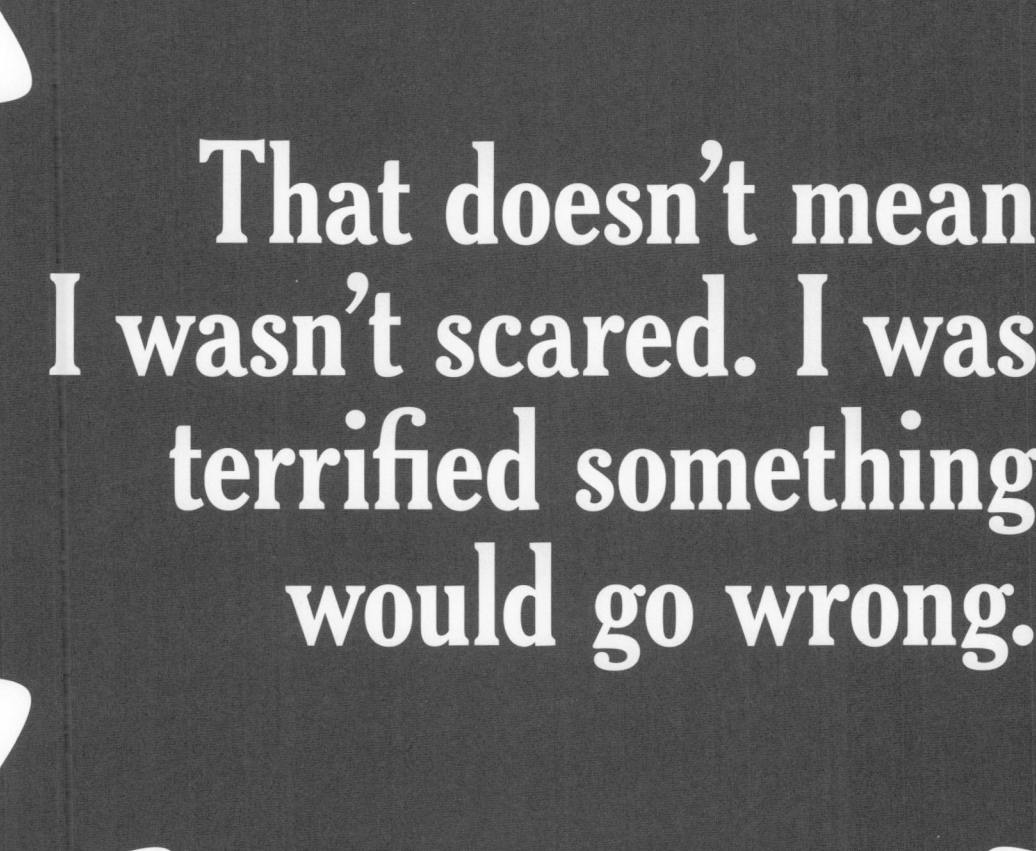

That doesn't mean I wasn't scared. I was terrified something would go wrong.

I cried with a counselor
and talked through my fears.

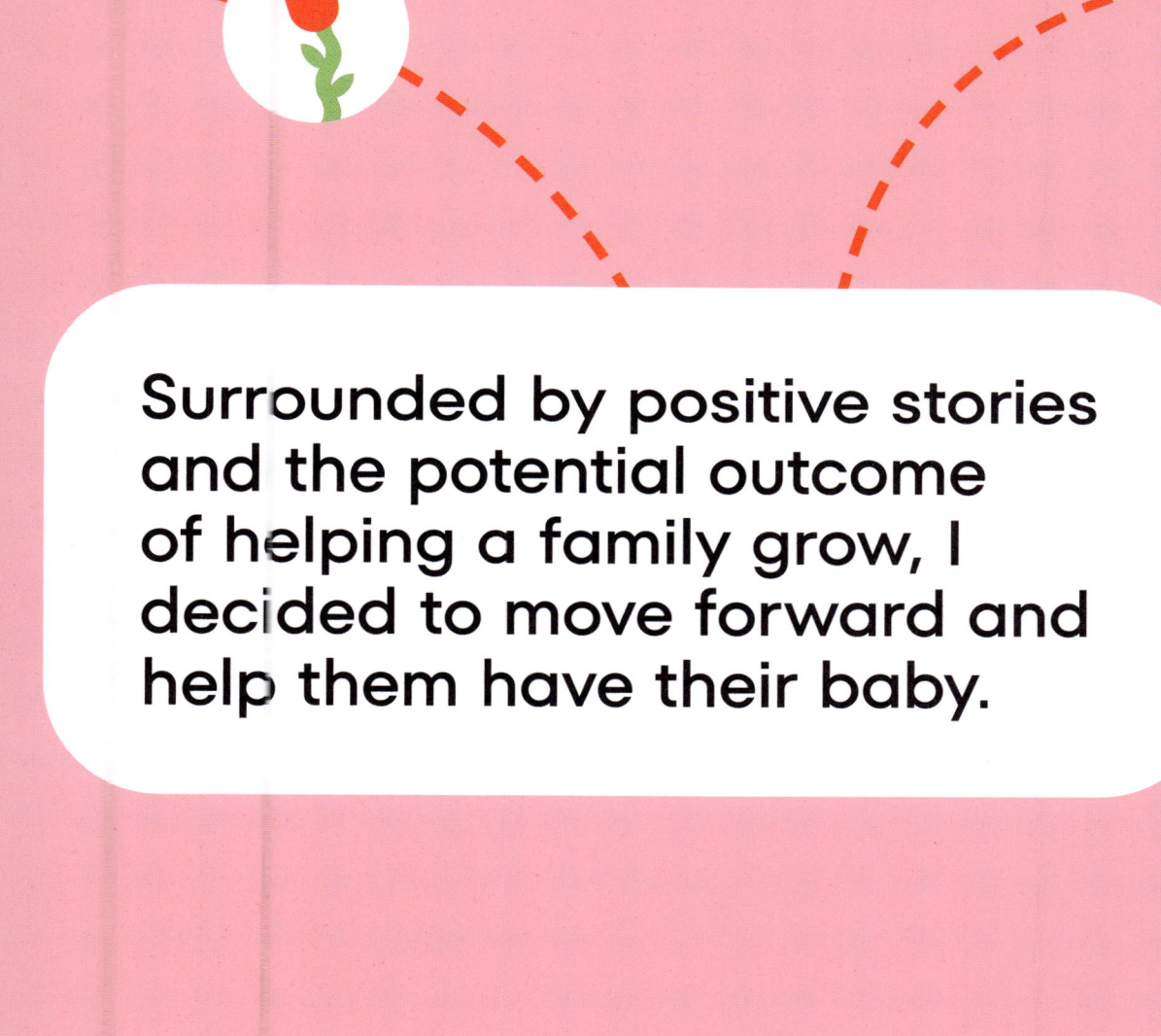

Surrounded by positive stories and the potential outcome of helping a family grow, I decided to move forward and help them have their baby.

And you might be won

dering about the baby!

The baby starts as a teeny tiny sperm and an itty bitty egg from the intended parents, and together, they create an embryo.

The embryo is kept in a special doctor's office called a fertility clinic—in a freezer for safekeeping.

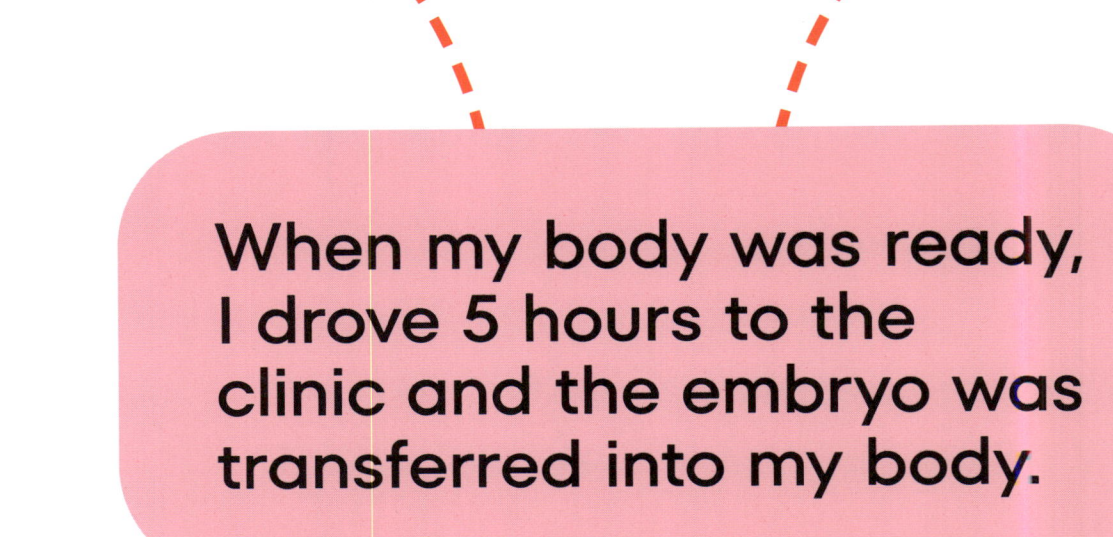

When my body was ready, I drove 5 hours to the clinic and the embryo was transferred into my body.

The whole procedure took less than 30 minutes, and it didn't hurt at all!

Next, we waited.

We waited 11 days before the doctors confirmed we were pregnant.
It felt like the longest 11 days ever!

And we found out around
the 4th of July, so we got
to celebrate with fireworks!

Just like any other pregnancy, I was a little sick and a little more tired than usual.

But overall, it was pretty easygoing (especially after the shots were all done).

The longer I was pregnant, the closer my relationship became with the baby's parents.

It was so fun to share all of their baby's milestones with them!

A question I got a lot was,

"How can you give up
the baby once they're born?"

I knew from the beginning
that this baby was theirs.

It was always about this family.
I got to share the good news of
my growing belly and every kick,
punch, and hiccup, and knew
it was their celebration.

Everything was leading up
to the baby's birthday,
and I was so excited.

They couldn't wait for the baby to come!

The day we went to the hospital was so fun and so full of love. It's still one of my favorite days!

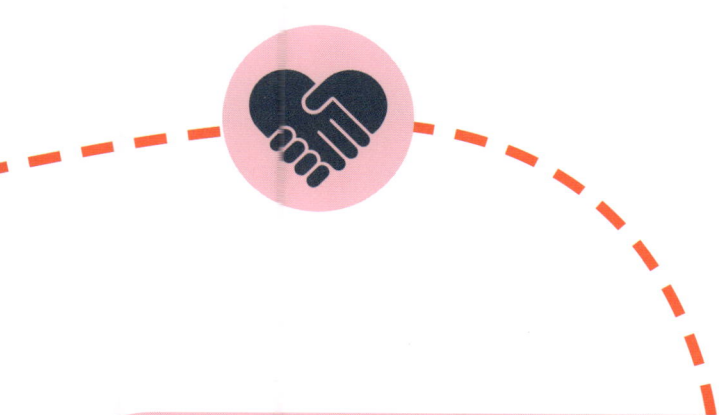

The nurses and doctors were there to help. My husband and the baby's parents were there to support me, and we laughed, told stories, and made jokes through the pain of labor and ultimately, delivery.

With my own kids,
I was an active participant
(obviously) in every experience.

But this time, I got to be a
witness to other people's
first moments as parents.

Their love grew so big, and it was inspiring to see!

The new parents cut the umbilical cord and got to snuggle, and stay up all night with their new baby (while I got to sleep!).

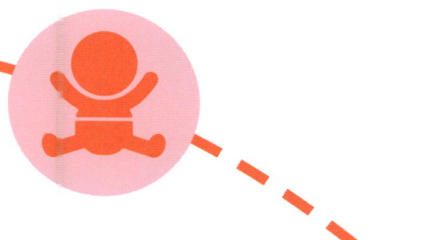

After we left the hospital, my kids got to meet the new baby.

This provided them with closure and a full understanding that the baby was safe and going to live a happy life with their family.

So, maybe you know someone who is a surrogate.

We take pride in carrying babies for people who cannot. For me, it was one of the most fulfilling experiences of my life to help someone achieve their dreams of having a baby.

And maybe you are a kid born by surrogacy.

Aside from your loving family, there's someone out there who cares for you and has big wishes for your future!

Your parents dreamed about you for years, and they love you more than you could ever imagine.

No matter whose belly you started out in, be sure to know one thing:

you are loved.

So dream big, go on adventures,
matter what, always do what

and do amazing things! And no
you can to help love grow.

Outro
for grownups

I imagine since you are reading this book, your life has been or will be positively influenced by a surrogate. And that is so cool! So here is what I recommend: share this book! Write notes in it. Start conversations with it. Share it with as many people as you can! As a surrogate, my husband and my kids were able to talk about (and talk to) the little surro babe inside my belly. We knew the intended parents well and had a close relationship. But our extended family, neighbors, friends, and acquaintances had so many questions! I was surprised by how invested people were in my story.

All of those people knew I was pregnant, but they didn't know all the details. And when they saw me again—without a baby—they had questions. People wondered and worried, asking me, "Where is the baby now?" But there is no reason to be concerned! This story is a happy one, and I want everyone to know that that baby is safe and happy in the arms of grownups who love them.

So tell your story! And then, share it with others!